Animal Pictures
Alphabetically With Names

Aa

Armadillo

Alpaca

Ankole-Watusi cattle

Anteater

Bb

Bison

Bat

Baboon

Bear

Cc

Chinchilla

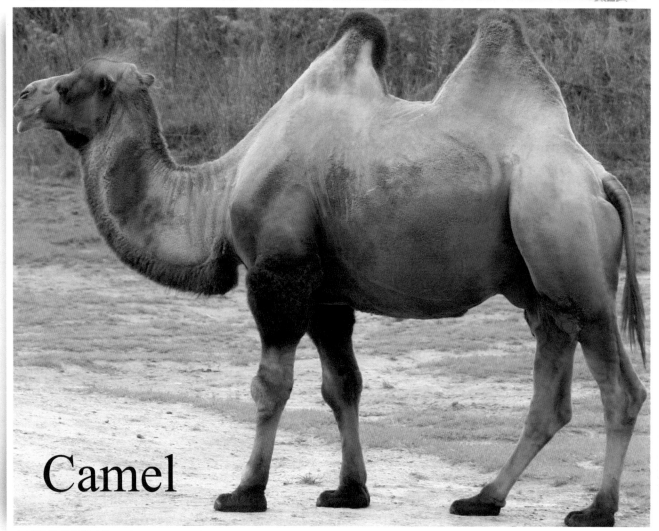

Camel

Chipmunk

Chameleon

Cheetah

Cow Highland

Crocodile

Dd

Donkey

Dog

Deer

Ee

Elephant

Ff

Ferret

Frog

Fox

Gg

Giraffe

Goat

Gorilla

Gila Monster

Gecko

Guinea Pig

Hh

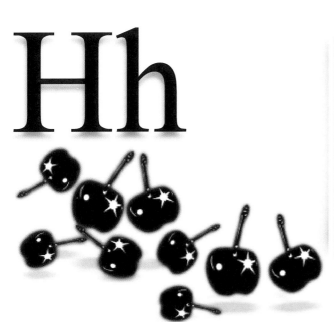

Hedgehog

Hyena

Horse

Hippopotamus

Ii

Ibex

Impala

Iguana

Jj

Jaguar

Kk

Koala

Kangaroo

L l

Leopard

Lemur

LION

Mm

Marmot

Meerkat

Monkey

Nn

Nutria

Nyala Antelope

Oo

Otter

Okapi

Orangutan

Pp

Panda

Pied Tamarin

Pig

Porcupine

Proboscis Monkey

Puma

Pony

Python

Qq

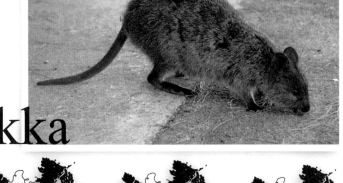

Quokka

Rr

Racoon

Ram

Reindeer

Rabbit

Rhinoceros

Ss

Seal

Sheep

Snake

Tt

Tortoise

Tamarin

Tarsier

Thorny Devil

Tapir

Tiger

Uu

Urial

Uakari Monkey

Vv

Vervet Monkey

Vole

Ww

Wallaby

Wildebeest

Warthog

Wolf

X x

Xerus

Yy

Yak

Zz

Zebu

Zebra

ALPACA	HEDGEHOG	PYTHON
ANKOLE-WATUSI	HIPPOPOTAMUS	QUOKKA
ANTEATER	HORSE	RABBIT
ARMADILLO	HYENA	RACOON
BABOON	IBEX	RAM
BAT	IGUANA	REINDEER
BEAR	IMPALA	RHINOCEROS
BISON	JAGUAR	SEAL
CAMEL	KANGAROO	SHEEP
CHAMELEON	KOALA	SNAKE
CHEETAH	LEMUR	TAMARIN MONKEY
CHINCHILLA	LEOPARD	TAPIR
CHIPMUNK	LION	TARSIER
COW HIGHLAND	MARMOT	THORNY DEVIL
CROCODILE	MEERKAT	TIGER
DEER	MONKEY	TORTOISE
DOG	NUTRIA	UAKARI MONKEY
DONKEY	NYALA ANTELOPE	URIAL
ELEPHANT	OKAPI	VERVET MONKEY
FERRET	ORANGUTAN	VOLE
FOX	OTTER	WALLABY
FROG	PANDA	WARTHOG
GECKO	PIED TAMARIN	WILDEBEEST
GILA MONSTER	PIG	WOLF
GIRAFFE	PONY	XERUS
GOAT	PORCUPINE	YAK
GORILLA	PROBOSCIS MONKEY	ZEBRA
GUINEA PIG	PUMA	ZEBU

Made in the USA
Lexington, KY
21 December 2011